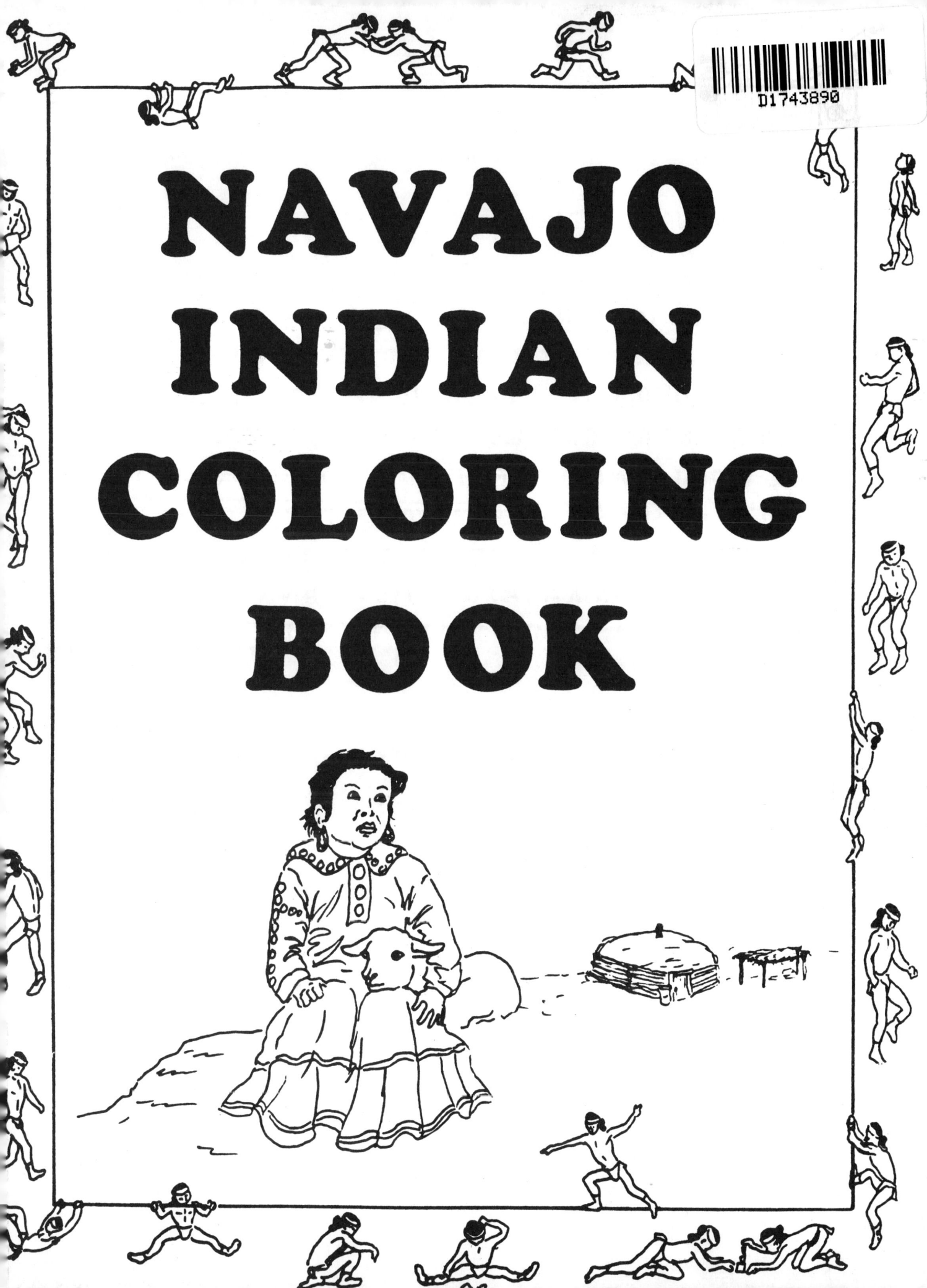

NAVAJO INDIAN COLORING BOOK

NAVAJO INDIAN COLORING BOOK

THE NAVAJO INDIANS LIVE ON A LARGE RESERVATION
IN THE STATES OF ARIZONA AND NEW MEXICO.
THESE PROUD, COLORFUL AND ARTISTIC PEOPLE ARE
GOOD SHEEP AND CATTLE RANCHERS AND FARMERS.
THE WOMEN WEAVE BEAUTIFUL WOOLEN RUGS. THEIR
BEAUTIFUL SILVER AND TURQUOISE JEWELRY IS
POPULAR ALL OVER THE WORLD. THERE ARE MANY
WORLD FAMOUS NAVAJO ARTISTS AND PAINTERS.
THEY ARE THE LARGEST INDIAN TRIBE IN THE
UNITED STATES.

DRAWINGS BY
CONNIE ASCH

ISBN 0-918080-06-1

TREASURE CHEST PUBLICATIONS, INC.
1842 W. Grant Road • Suite 107
P. O. Box 5250
Tucson, AZ 85703
(602) 623-9558

HAVING A LUNCH OF COFFEE, FRYBREAD AND MUTTON STEW

NAVAJO SILVERSMITHS MAKE BEAUTIFUL JEWELRY

NAVAJO WOMAN SHEEPHERDER

A NAVAJO INDIAN GIRL HERDING SHEEP
IN A SNOWSTORM

A NAVAJO INDIAN WOMAN AND THREE BABIES

NAVAJO INDIAN WOMEN SHEARING SHEEP FOR WOOL TO MAKE RUGS

NAVAJO WOMEN
CARDING WOOL
BEFORE SPINNING IT
INTO YARN

A NAVAJO INDIAN WOMAN SPINNING
WOOL INTO YARN

NAVAJO WOMAN SPINNING YARN IN FRONT OF A SUMMER HOGAN

NAVAJO INDIAN WOMEN WEAVE COLORFUL RUGS
USUALLY OUT IN THE OPEN

NAVAJO HOGAN AND DESERT SHOWER

MAKING FRYBREAD

DAYDREAMING ON THE CANYON RIM

AN INITIATION CEREMONY
MEANS A MUD BATH

A NAVAJO INDIAN HORSE RACE

FIVE NAVAJO BOYS ON A STUBBORN BURRO

A NAVAJO INDIAN FOOTRACE

NAVAJO GIRL CATCHING A PARTNER FOR THE SQUAW DANCE

BUYING GROCERIES AT THE TRADING POST

A NAVAJO MEDICINE MAN
DOING A SANDPAINTING
FOR A CURING CEREMONY

A NAVAJO YEBICHI DANCE

NAVAJO WOMEN COMING FROM THE TRADING POST

A NAVAJO FAMILY GOING TO A GATHERING
CALLED A "SING"

A NAVAJO GIRL BRINGING WOOD TO THE HOGAN
FOR THE FIRE

A NAVAJO INDIAN PREPARING TO TAKE A SWEAT BATH

A NAVAJO INDIAN WOMAN BAKING BREAD
IN AN OUTDOOR OVEN

A NAVAJO INDIAN MAKING FIRE BY FRICTION

DRAWING A MAP IN THE SAND

GRANDFATHER TELLS
INTERESTING STORIES